THE GOAT
or
WHO IS SYLVIA?

ALSO BY EDWARD ALBEE

The Zoo Story

The Death of Bessie Smith

The Sandbox

Fam and Yam

The American Dream

Who's Afraid of Virginia Woolf?

The Ballad of the Sad Café

Tiny Alice

Malcolm

A Delicate Balance

Everything in the Garden

Box and *Quotations from Mao Tse-Tung*

All Over

Seascape

Listening

Counting the Ways

The Lady from Dubuque

The Man Who Had Three Arms

Marriage Play

Finding the Sun

Three Tall Women

Fragments—A Concerto Grosso

The Play about the Baby

Occupant

THE GOAT

or

WHO IS SYLVIA?

(Notes toward a definition of tragedy)

Edward Albee

THE OVERLOOK PRESS
WOODSTOCK & NEW YORK

First published in paperback in the United States in 2005 by
The Overlook Press, Peter Mayer Publishers, Inc.
Woodstock & New York

WOODSTOCK:
One Overlook Drive
Woodstock, NY 12498
www.overlookpress.com
[for individual orders, bulk and special sales, contact our Woodstock office]

NEW YORK:
141 Wooster Street
New York, NY 10012

Library of Congress Cataloging-in-Publication Data

Albee, Edward, 1928–
The goat or who is Sylvia? / by Edward Albee.
p. cm.
1. Architects—Drama. 2. Married people—Drama.
3. Gay youth—Drama. 4. Goats—Drama I. Title

PS3551.L25 G63 2003   812'.54 21   2003042090

Book design and type formatting by Bernard Schleifer
Manufactured in the United States of America
FIRST EDITION
3 5 7 9 8 6 4 2
ISBN 1-58567-647-0

For Liz McCann
—because

The Goat had its world premiere in New York City on March 10, 2002, at the Golden Theatre, produced by Elizabeth Ireland McCann, Daryl Roth, Carole Shorenstein Hays, Terry Allen Kramer, Scott Rudin, Bob Boyett, Scott Nederlander, and Sine/ZPI. It was directed by David Esbjornson, with the following cast:

Stevie	*Mercedes Ruehl*
Martin	*Bill Pullman*
Ross	*Stephen Rowe*
Billy	*Jeffrey Carlson*

The scenic design was by John Arnone, costume design by Elizabeth Hope Clancy, lighting design by Kenneth Posner, and sound design by Mark Bennett. The production stage manager was Erica Schwartz. The general manager was Joey Parnes. The company manager was Elizabeth Blitzer. The casting was done by Bernard Telsey Casting. The press representative was Sam Rudy of Shirley Herz Associates.

On September 13, 2002, the roles of Stevie and Martin were taken over by Sally Field and Bill Irwin, respectively.

Scene One

(The living room)
*(*STEVIE *onstage, arranging flowers)*

STEVIE
(Calling offstage) What time are they coming? *(No response)*
Martin? What time are they coming?

MARTIN
(Offstage) What? *(Entering)* What?

STEVIE
(A little smile; a slowish statement) What . . . time . . . are . . .
they . . . coming.

MARTIN
Who? *(Recalling)* Oh! Oh. *(Looks at watch)* Soon; very soon.
Why can't I remember anything?

STEVIE
(Finishing flowers) Why can't you remember?

MARTIN
Anything; nothing; can't remember a thing. This morning—so
far!—I couldn't remember where I'd put the new head for the

razor; I couldn't recall Ross's son's name—still can't; two cards in my jacket make no sense to me whatever, and I'm not sure I know why I came in here.

STEVIE

Todd.

MARTIN

What?

STEVIE

Ross's son is called Todd.

MARTIN

(*Slaps his forehead*) Right! Why the flowers?

STEVIE

To brighten up the corner . . .

MARTIN

. . . where you *are*? Where *I* am?

STEVIE

. . . where you'll probably be sitting, to make the cameras happy.

MARTIN

(*Smelling the flowers*) What are they?

STEVIE

Cameras?

MARTIN

No; these.

STEVIE

Ranunculus. I (*Then*) I: ranunculi.

MARTIN

Pretty. Why don't they smell?

STEVIE

They're secretive; probably too subtle for your forgetful nose.

MARTIN

(*Shakes his head, mock concern*) Every sense going! Taste next! Touch; hearing. Hah! Hearing!

STEVIE

What?

MARTIN

What?

STEVIE

And to think you're only fifty. Did you find it?

MARTIN

What?

STEVIE

The new head for the razor.

MARTIN

Right! A new head! I'll need that next—the whole thing.

STEVIE

Why did you want to remember Todd's name?

MARTIN

Well, to begin with, I shouldn't be forgetting it, and when Ross shows up and he asks about Billy I can't say "He's fine; how's . . . you know . . . *your* son . . . "

STEVIE

Todd.

MARTIN

Todd. "How's old Todd?"

STEVIE

Young Todd.

MARTIN

Yes. It's the little slips.

STEVIE

I wouldn't worry about it. Are you going to offer them stuff? Coffee? Beer?

MARTIN

(*Preoccupied*) Probably. Do you think it means anything?

STEVIE

I don't know what "it" is.

MARTIN

That I can't remember anything.

STEVIE

Probably not: you have too much to remember, that's all. You could go in for a checkup . . . if you can remember our doctor's name.

MARTIN

(*Nailing it*) Percy!

STEVIE

Right!

MARTIN

(*To himself*) Who could forget that? Nobody has a doctor named Percy. (*To* STEVIE) What's the matter with me?

STEVIE

You're fifty.

MARTIN

No; more than that.

STEVIE

The old foreboding? The sense that everything going right is a sure sign that everything's going wrong, of all the awful to come? All that?

MARTIN

(*Rueful*) Probably. Why did I come in here?

STEVIE

I heard you in the hall; I called you.

MARTIN

Aha.

STEVIE

What's my *name*?

MARTIN

Pardon?

STEVIE

Who *am* I? Who am *I*?

MARTIN

(*Acted*) You're the love of my life, the mother of my handsome and worrisome son, my playmate, my cook, my bottlewasher. Do you?

STEVIE

What?

MARTIN

Wash my bottles?

STEVIE

(*Puzzles it*) Not as a habit. I may have—washed one of your bottles. Do you have bottles?

MARTIN

Everyone has bottles.

STEVIE

Right. But what's my *name*?

MARTIN

(*Pretending confusion*) Uh . . . Stevie?

STEVIE

Good. Will this be a long one?

MARTIN

A long what?

STEVIE

Interview.

MARTIN

The usual, I guess. Ross said it wasn't going to be a feature—
sort of a catch-up.

STEVIE

On your fiftieth.

MARTIN

(*Nods*) On my fiftieth. I wonder if I should tell him that my
mind's going? If I can remember.

STEVIE

(*Laughs; hugs him from behind*) Your mind's not going.

MARTIN

My what?

STEVIE

Your mind, darling; it's not going . . . anywhere.

MARTIN

(*Serious*) Am I too young for Alzheimer's?

STEVIE

Probably. Isn't it nice to be too young for something?

MARTIN

(*Mind elsewhere*) Um-hum.

STEVIE

The joke is, if you can remember what it's called you don't
have it.

MARTIN

Have what?

STEVIE

Alz . . . (*they both laugh; he kisses her forehead*) Oh, you know how to turn a girl on! Forehead kisses! (*Sniffs him*) Where have you been?

MARTIN

(*Releases her; preoccupied*) What time are they coming?

STEVIE

Soon, you said; very soon.

MARTIN

I did? Good.

STEVIE

Did you find it?

MARTIN

What?

STEVIE

The head for your razor.

MARTIN

No; it's around somewhere. (*Fishes in a pocket, brings out cards*) But these! Now these! What the hell are these!? "Basic Services, Limited." Basic Services, Limited?? Limited to what!? (*The other card*) "Clarissa Atherton." (*Shrugs*) Clarissa Atherton? No number, no . . . internet thing? Clarissa Atherton?

STEVIE

Basic services? Clarissa Atherton, basic services?

MARTIN

Hm? Every time someone gives me one of these, I know I'm supposed to give them one back, and I don't have them. It's embarrassing.

STEVIE

I've told you to have them made . . . cards.

MARTIN

I don't want to.

STEVIE

Then don't. Who is she?

MARTIN

Who?

STEVIE

Clarissa Atherton, basic services. Does she smell funny?

MARTIN

I don't know. (*Afterthought*) I don't know who she is, as far as
I know. Where were we this week?

STEVIE

(*Overly casual; stretches*) Oh, it doesn't matter sweetie. If
you're seeing this Atherton woman, this . . . dominatrix . . .
who smells funny . . .

MARTIN

How could I be seeing her—whoever she is? There's nothing
on the card. Dominatrix!?

STEVIE

Why not?

MARTIN

Maybe you know things I don't.

STEVIE

Maybe.

MARTIN

And I probably know one or two things you *don't*.

STEVIE

It evens out.

MARTIN

Yes. Do I look OK?

STEVIE

For the TV? Yes.

MARTIN

Yes. (*Turning*) Really?

STEVIE

I said: yes; fine. (*Indicates*) The old prep school tie?

MARTIN

(*Genuine, as he looks*) Is it? Oh, yeah; so it is.

STEVIE

(*Not letting him have it*) *No* one puts on their prep school tie by accident. *No* one.

MARTIN

(*Considers*) What if you can't remember that's what it is?

STEVIE

No one!! If you do get Alzheimer's, and you get to the stage you don't know who *I* am, who *Billy* is, who *you* are, for that matter . . .

MARTIN

Billy?

STEVIE

(*Laughs*) Stop it! When you get to the point you can't re-member anything, someone will hand you *that* (*indicates his tie*) and you'll look at it and you'll say (*terrible imitation of aged man*) "Ahhhhh! My prep school tie! My prep school tie!"

(*They chuckle; the doorbell rings/chimes*)

MARTIN

Ah! Doom time!

STEVIE

(*Quite matter of fact*) If you *are* seeing that woman, I think we'd better talk about it.

MARTIN

(*Stops. Long pause; matter of fact*) If I *were* . . . we *would*.

STEVIE

(*As offhand as possible*) If not the dominatrix, then some blonde half your age, some . . . chippie, as they used to call them . . .

MARTIN

. . . or, worst of all, someone just like you? As bright; as resourceful; as intrepid; . . . merely . . . new?

STEVIE

(*Warm smile; shake of head*) You win 'em all, don't you.

MARTIN

(*Same smile*) Enough.

(*Door again. The next several speeches are done in a greatly exaggerated Noel Coward manner: English accents, flamboyant gestures*)

STEVIE

Something's going on, isn't it!?

MARTIN

Yes! I've fallen in love!

STEVIE

I knew it!

MARTIN

Hopelessly!

STEVIE

I knew it!

MARTIN

I fought against it!

STEVIE

Oh, you poor darling!

MARTIN

Fought hard!

STEVIE

I suppose you'd better tell me!

MARTIN

I can't! I can't!

STEVIE

Tell me! Tell me!

MARTIN

Her name is Sylvia!

STEVIE

Sylvia? Who is Sylvia?

MARTIN

She's a goat; Sylvia is a goat! (*Acting manner dropped; normal tone now; serious, flat*) She's a goat.

STEVIE

(*Long pause; she stares, finally smiles. She giggles, chortles, moves toward the hall; normal tone*) You're too much! (*Exits*)

MARTIN

I am? (*Shrugs; to himself*) You try to *tell* them; you try to be *honest*. What do they do? They laugh at you. (*Imitation*) "You're too much!" (*Thinks about it*) I suppose I am.

ROSS

Hey honey.

STEVIE

Hi Ross. (ROSS *enters with* STEVIE)

ROSS

Hello there, old man!

MARTIN

I'm fifty!

ROSS

It's a term of endearment. Nice flowers.

MARTIN

It is?

ROSS

What? What is?

MARTIN

"Hello there, old man." Ranunculi.

ROSS

Pardon?

STEVIE

The proper plural of ranunculus—the flowers, according to old Martin here.

MARTIN

Some say ranunculuses, but that sounds wrong, even though it's probably perfectly acceptable.

ROSS

(*Not interested*) Aha! Let's move that chair over to the . . . whatever they are . . . the flowers. (*To* MARTIN) Are you happy in that chair?

MARTIN

Am I happy in it? I don't even know if I've ever sat in it. (*To* STEVIE) Have I? Have I ever sat in it?

STEVIE

You just did, and you sat in it the last time Ross did the program with you.

ROSS

That's *right*!

MARTIN

Yes . . . but was I happy? Did I sit there and did contentment bathe me in its warm light?

ROSS

You got me, fella.

STEVIE

Yes; contentment fell; you sat there and I watched it bathe you in its warm light. I've got to go.

MARTIN

Where are you going?

STEVIE

(*No information*) Out.

MARTIN

Are we in tonight?

STEVIE

Yes. I think Billy's going out.

MARTIN

Naturally!

STEVIE

We're in. (*Glee*) TV time! I'm getting my hair done, and then I thought I'd stop by the feed store. (*Exits, giggling*)

ROSS

By *what*? She's going to stop by *what*?

MARTIN

(*Staring after her*) Nothing; nowhere. (*To* ROSS) No crew?

ROSS

Just me this time—the old hand-held. (*Indicates camera*) You ready for the chair?

MARTIN

(*Sing-song*) Ha, ha. (*Suddenly remembering*) How's old *Todd*!?

ROSS

"Old Todd?"

MARTIN

You know: old *Todd*!

ROSS

You mean my baby son who just last week it seems I dandled on my knee? *That* old Todd?

MARTIN

Lovely word—dandled. Yes: *that* old Todd.

ROSS

Who I cannot accept having become eighteen?

MARTIN

Whom.

ROSS

Maybe.

MARTIN

Yes; that one. Can any of us? Ever?

ROSS

Pushing me further into middle age?

MARTIN

Yes; that one.

ROSS

(*Offhand*) He's OK. (*Laughs*) He asked me last week—first time since he was four, or something—why he didn't have a brother, or a sister, or whatever—why April and I never had another kid.

MARTIN

April, May, June—the pastel months. You name girl babies after them.

ROSS

(*Doesn't care*) Right. (*Does care*) I told him if you do it right the first time, why take a chance on another.

MARTIN

Did he like that one?

ROSS

Seemed to. Of course, I could have told him the whole graduating class got together and vowed that we would all have only one kid each—keep the population down. Speaking of which, how's Billy? How's *yours*—*your* one and only?

MARTIN

(*Attempted throw-away tone*) Ohhhh, seventeen last week—didn't Todd come to the party? No, I guess he didn't. Real cute kid, Billy, bright as you'd ever want, gay as the nineties.

ROSS

Passing phase. Have you had the old serious talk?

MARTIN

The "You'll get over it once you meet the right girl" lecture? Nah, I'm too smart for that, so's he, so's Billy. I told him to be sure. Says he's sure; loves it, he says.

ROSS

Well, of course he loves it; he's getting laid, for God's sake! Don't worry about him.

MARTIN

Who?

ROSS

Billy! Seventeen; it's a phase.

MARTIN

Like the moon, eh?

ROSS

He'll straighten out—to make a pun. (*To quash the subject*)
Billy'll come out of it; he'll be OK.

MARTIN

(*Reassuring if a bit patronizing*) Sure.

ROSS

Voice test? Phone off?

MARTIN

I assume Stevie did it.

ROSS

I hear a kind of . . . rushing sound, like a . . . wooooosh!, or
. . . wings, or something.

MARTIN

It's probably the Eumenides.

ROSS

More like the dishwasher. There; it stopped.

MARTIN

Then it probably wasn't the Eumenides: they don't stop.

ROSS

(*Agreeing*) They go right on.

MARTIN

Right.

ROSS

Why is Stevie going to the feed store?

MARTIN

She isn't.

ROSS

Then why did she . . .

MARTIN

It's a joke.

ROSS

A standing joke?

MARTIN

No, a new one; a brand-new one.

ROSS

OK? Ready? Ready Martin; here we go; just . . . be yourself.

MARTIN

Really?

ROSS

(*A tiny bit testy*) Well, no; maybe not. Put on your public face.

MARTIN

(*Overly cheerful*) OK!!

ROSS

And don't switch in the middle.

MARTIN

(*More*) OK!!

ROSS

(*Under his breath*) Jesus! (*Announcer voice*) Good evening. This is Ross Tuttle. Welcome to People Who Matter. Some people have birthdays and no one pays them any mind. Well

. . . family, of course, friends. And others . . . well, some people are . . . I was going to say special, but that's a . . . dumb word, for everyone matters, everyone's special. But some people matter in extraordinary ways, in ways which affect the lives of the rest of us—enrich them, inform them. Some people, I guess, are, well . . . more extraordinary than others. Martin Gray—whom you've met on this program before—is such a man, such a person. Good evening, Martin.

MARTIN

Good . . . uh, evening, Ross. (*sotto voce*) It's mid-afternoon.

ROSS

(*Quiet snarl*) I know. Shut up! (*Announcer voice*) Three things happened to you this week, Martin. You became the youngest person ever to win the Pritzker Prize, architecture's version of the Nobel. Also this week you were chosen to design The World City, the two hundred billion dollar dream city of the future, financed by U.S. electronics technology and set to rise in the wheatfields of our Middle West. Also, this week, you celebrated your fiftieth birthday. Happy birthday, Martin, and congratulations!

MARTIN

(*Brief pause; casual*) Thanks, Ross.

ROSS

Quite a week, Martin!

MARTIN

(*A little puzzled*) Yes; yes it was. Quite a week.

ROSS

(*Big*) How does it feel, Martin?

MARTIN

Becoming fifty?

ROSS

(*Pushing*) No. *All* of it. Yes.

MARTIN

Well . . .

ROSS

(*Sensing no answer is coming*) It must be amazing! No, thrilling!

MARTIN

Turning fifty? No: not really.

ROSS

(*Not amused*) No! The other! The World City! The Pritzker! All that!

MARTIN

(*Genuine surprise*) Oh, that! Well, yes . . . amazing, thrilling.

ROSS

(*Prompting*) For one so young.

MARTIN

(*Innocent*) Fifty is young?

ROSS

(*Controlling himself*) For the Pritzker Prize! Where were you when they told you?

MARTIN

I was at the gym; I'd taken all my clothes off, and Stevie called me there.

ROSS

Stevie is your wife.

MARTIN

I know that.

ROSS

How did it make you feel?

MARTIN

Stevie being my wife?

ROSS

No: the Prize.

MARTIN

Well, it was . . . gratifying—not being naked, but . . . hearing about it—the Prize.

ROSS

(*Exuberant*) Weren't you . . . thunderstruck!?

MARTIN

Well, no; they'd hinted at it—the Prize, I mean, and . . .

ROSS

(*Heavily prompting*) But it was pretty wonderful, wasn't it?

MARTIN

(*Understanding what to say*) Yes; yes it was pretty wonder-ful—*is* pretty wonderful.

ROSS

Tell us about The World City.

MARTIN

Well, you just *did:* two hundred billion dollars, and all, the wheatfields of Kansas, or whatever . . .

ROSS

What an honor! What a duo of honors! You're at the . . . pinnacle of your success, Martin . . .

MARTIN

(*Considers that*) You mean it's all downhill from here?

ROSS

CUT! CUT! (*Camera down. To* MARTIN) What's the matter with you!?

MARTIN

Sorry?

ROSS

I can't shoot that! You were a million miles away!!

MARTIN

(*Considering*) That far.

ROSS

You want to try again?

MARTIN

Try what?

ROSS

The taping! The program!

MARTIN

(*As if seeing the camera for the first time*) Oooooh.

ROSS

We're taping!

MARTIN

(*Unhappy*) Yes; I know.

ROSS

(*Nicely concerned*) Something the matter?

MARTIN

I think so. Yes; probably.

ROSS

Do you want to talk about it, as they say?

MARTIN

About what?

ROSS

About what's the matter.

MARTIN

(*Concerned*) Why? What's the matter?

ROSS

You said something was the matter, that you think something's the matter.

MARTIN

(*Far away*) Oh.

ROSS

Forty years, Martin; we've known each other forty years— since we were ten.

MARTIN

(*Trying to understand*) Yes. That gives you something? Rights, or something?

ROSS

I'm your oldest friend.

MARTIN

No; my aesthetics professor at college; I still see him; he's a lot older than you; he's over ninety.

ROSS

(*So patient*) Your longest friend: the person you've known the longest.

MARTIN

No; my Aunt Sarah; she's known me . . .

ROSS

(*Trying to stay patient*) She's not a friend!

MARTIN

(*Deep, quiet surprise*) Oh?

ROSS

(*Close to giving up*) No; she's a relative; relatives are not friends!

MARTIN

Oh, now . . .

ROSS

Are not the same as friends. Jesus!

MARTIN

Aha! Yes; well, you're right. I've known you longer as a friend than anyone. (*Tiny pause*) Why is that relevant?

ROSS

Because you're troubled, and I thought that as your oldest friend I might be able to . . .

MARTIN

I am? Is that true?

ROSS

You said that something was the matter!

MARTIN

(*Not remembering*) I did, hunh?

ROSS

Why are you so . . . ? (*Can't find the word*)

MARTIN

Are you still shooting? Are you still on?

ROSS

(*Heavy sigh*) No. We'll try to do it at the studio later. Sorry.

MARTIN

Can I get up now?

ROSS

If you want to; if you're not happy.

MARTIN

Why are you talking to me like I was a child?

ROSS

Because you're acting like one.

MARTIN

(*Innocent*) I am?

ROSS

Probably the most important week of your life . . .

MARTIN

(*Impressed, if uninvolved*) Really!

ROSS

. . . and you act like you don't know whether you're coming or going, like you don't know where you are.

MARTIN

(*Self-absorbed, almost to himself*) Maybe it's . . . love or something.

ROSS

Maybe what is?

MARTIN

Like a child.

ROSS

(*Bingo!*) You're having an affair!

MARTIN

SHHHHHHHH! I mean, Jesus!

ROSS

(*Shrugs*) It's OK; he's not having an affair.

MARTIN

Jesus! Too bad you didn't bring the crew; they'd love this.

ROSS

(*Cool*) They know their business.

MARTIN

And . . . ?

ROSS

And . . . ?

MARTIN

Aren't you guys friendly anymore?

ROSS

They know their business. What do you want me to do—have them over for *dinner*? Have every crew over for dinner?

MARTIN

(*Puzzled*) No, I guess not. (*Afterthought*) Why *not*?

ROSS

Hm?

MARTIN

Why *not* have them over for dinner?

ROSS

Oh, for God's sake, Martin!

MARTIN

(*Hands up, defensively*) Ok! OK! Jesus!

ROSS

It's just that . . . it's just that I don't . . . mix with . . .

MARTIN

(*Joyful*) The *help*?! You don't mix with the *help*!?

ROSS

What *is* wrong with you today!? That's not what I meant, and you *know* it.

MARTIN

(*Half-serious, half-joking*) You're a snob! I guess I've always known that. For all your left-wing, proletarian background, you're a *snob*: worst kind.

ROSS

(*A plea; a warning*) We're best friends, remember?

MARTIN

Meaning . . . ?

ROSS

We like each other.

MARTIN

(*"So, that's it!"*) Ohhhhhhhh!

ROSS

More than anyone.

MARTIN

(*Ibid*) Ohhhhh! (*Considers it*) Right; yes. Who else can I be cranky with?

ROSS

Stevie??

MARTIN

Ya know, Stevie doesn't take too well to cranky anymore. If she's developed a flaw, it's that. "Don't be so cranky, Martin."

ROSS

Pity.
(*They've gentled down now*)

MARTIN

(*Shrugs*) Well . . . *you* know.

ROSS

(*Pause*) So you're in love.

MARTIN

With Stevie? Sure! Twenty-two years now.

ROSS

No, I mean . . . "in love." Ficky-fack! Humpty-doodle!

MARTIN

What on earth are you talking about!? "Humpty-doodle!?"

ROSS

You said you were in love—outside of Stevie, as I read it.

MARTIN

(*Genuine*) Really? I don't remember.

ROSS

(*Impatient sigh; abrupt*) O . . . K! That does it!

MARTIN

(*As Ross gathers up stuff; true innocence*) Where are you going?

ROSS

(*Staring him down*) I'm gathering my things and I'm taking my left-wing . . . what was it?

MARTIN

Uh . . . proletarian.

ROSS

. . . proletarian self outa here.

MARTIN

"But, why!" as the . . .

ROSS

Look, I came here to fucking interview you.

MARTIN

Fine.

ROSS

To boost your ego even more than . . .

MARTIN

I have no ego.

ROSS

Bullshit! Even more than where it is already and you fuck that up.

MARTIN

Fine. You say fuck a lot.

ROSS

You say fine a lot. (*He laughs; so does* MARTIN)

MARTIN

Words beginning with F.

ROSS

(*Smiles*) Yeah. (*Pause*) So; tell me about it.

MARTIN

(*Shy*) About . . . ?

ROSS

(*Gently urging*) Your new love.

MARTIN

Oh; that.

ROSS

Yes.

MARTIN

I don't know that I want to.

ROSS

Yes; you do.

MARTIN

. . . that I can.

ROSS

Try.

MARTIN

(*Small smile*) You're persistent.

ROSS

Best friend. (MARTIN *tries to talk; can't*) Best friend.

MARTIN

(*Frustrated explosion*) OK!! OK!! (*Heavy, slow sigh; long pause*) I don't know if I ever thought that . . . well, that Stevie and I would be . . . well, no; we're not. (*Pause*)

ROSS

Are you telling me about it?

MARTIN

I'm starting to . . . or maybe I'm beginning to start.

ROSS

Oh; OK.

MARTIN

As I said, it never occurred to me that anything like this would come up. 'Cause we've always been good together—good in bed, good out; always honest, always . . . considerate. I've not been unfaithful our whole marriage; I want you to know this; never physically untrue, as they say.

ROSS

That's amazing. It's wonderful, but . . . wow!

MARTIN

Yes: wow. Oh, I've been groped in the kitchen by a cutie or two, late, a party, once or twice, and I've had my hand a couple of places a couple of times, but I've never . . . *done* anything. You follow.

ROSS

Yes; I follow.

MARTIN

It never seemed . . . well, necessary, either to be able to do a
comparison, or . . . even for its own sake. I never needed it, I
guess. Do you remember that time, that college reunion
weekend you and I decided to call that service they'd told us
about . . . the gang had told us about?

ROSS

(*Rueful laugh*) The Ladies Aid Society?

MARTIN

Yeah, and you called them, and . . .

ROSS

. . . and we had a couple of bimbos over . . .

MARTIN

Bimbi.

ROSS

Yes? (*Broad*) Ohhhhh, I remember.

MARTIN

. . . and you were married already, and Stevie and I were dat-
ing . . . or going together . . .

ROSS

. . . or whatever.

MARTIN

Yes.

ROSS

(*Trying to recall*) What were their names?

MARTIN

Mine was Alice.

ROSS

Big girl.

MARTIN

Large Alice.

ROSS

Right! Mine was Trudy, or Trixie, or . . .

MARTIN

April.

ROSS

Yes? April?

MARTIN

Yes; April.

ROSS

(*Interior*) Oh, shit; April's called April.

MARTIN

(*Registering it*) Yes; she is.

ROSS

Shit. (*Pause; recovers*) And we had them up to our room—two beds, two hookers.

MARTIN

Just like when we roomed together.

ROSS

A kind of reunion for the reunion.

MARTIN

Yes, I guess so. And do you remember what happened?

ROSS

I don't know. What happened?

MARTIN

I couldn't do it? Couldn't perform?

ROSS

(*Recalls*) Oh, yeah. You'd never had that problem when we were undergrads! I'd be pumping away, you pumping away in the next bed.

MARTIN

I hadn't met Stevie.

ROSS

(*Soberer*) Right.

MARTIN

That night at the reunion with large Alice . . .

ROSS

You were going with Stevie . . .

MARTIN

Right.

ROSS

I remember.

MARTIN

I don't know why I ever thought I wanted to . . . *you* know.

ROSS

No. Right.

MARTIN

I was already in love with Stevie and I didn't know how much.

ROSS

(*A little deriding*) Amazing theory: the heart rules the dick. I always thought that the dick was driven by . . .

MARTIN

Don't be cynical.

ROSS

Oh, a new part of my left-wing . . . what?

MARTIN

Proletarian.

ROSS

Yes. My left-wing, proletarian, snobbish, *cynical* self.

MARTIN

Right, and not new. (*They both smile*) You *do* see, don't you?
In love with Stevie, she owns every part of me. Look, when
I'm traveling, and Stevie's *here*, and I get itchy . . .

ROSS

You give yourself a handjob and you think about Stevie—
about you and Stevie.

MARTIN

(*Shy*) Yes.

ROSS

(*Shakes his head; noncommittal*) Wonderful.

MARTIN

I didn't catch your tone.

ROSS

There wasn't any. Go on; how did you fuck it up?

MARTIN

(*Truly confused*) What? Fuck *what* up?

ROSS

Are you playing games?

MARTIN

No. Fuck *what* up?

ROSS

(*Serious*) Your life, apparently—you and Stevie. How'd you
fuck it up?

MARTIN

(*Pause*) Oh. (*Pause*) That.

ROSS

(*Impatient*) Getting an answer out of you . . .

MARTIN

OK! OK! As I told you, I've never been unfaithful, never needed it . . . never . . .

ROSS

Yeah, yeah; right. You told me.

MARTIN

And then . . . one day . . . (*Stops*)

ROSS

(*After a silence*) Yeah!?

MARTIN

And then one day. (*Says nothing more*)

ROSS

(*Long pause*) That's it!?

MARTIN

(*Goes ahead*) And then one day . . . one day . . . well, I was house-hunting—barn hunting, actually. Stevie and I had decided it was time to have a real country place—a farm, maybe— we deserved it. So, I was in the car about sixty miles out from the city. Stevie couldn't come with me.

ROSS

Beyond the suburbs.

MARTIN

Yes; beyond the suburbs. Farms around it, small farms. And I found a wonderful place, a wonderful old farmhouse, and a lot of land.

ROSS

The old back twenty, or whatever it is.

MARTIN

Right! Whatever. And I called Stevie, and told her she had to see it, and I'd put a hold on it 'til she could see it. And Stevie was . . . well, "A farm?" she said, but I said "Wait!" And the real estate guy was OK with that for a while. And I was driving out of the town back to the highway, and I stopped at the top of a hill.

ROSS

Crest.

MARTIN

Right. And I stopped, and the view was . . . well, not spectacular, but . . . wonderful. Fall, you know?, with leaves turning and the town below me and great scudding clouds and those country smells.

ROSS

Cow shit, and all that.

MARTIN

(*Broad country parody*) New-mown hay, fella! The smell a country; the smell a apples! (*Normal tone again*) The roadside stands, with corn and other stuff piled high, and baskets full of other things—beans and tomatoes and those great white peaches you only get late summer . . .

ROSS

(*Broad*) The whole thing; right.

MARTIN

(*Shakes his head*) Oh, you city boys! And from up there I could trace the roads out toward the farm, and it gave me a kind of shiver.

ROSS

The ludicrous often does.

MARTIN

Anyway . . .

ROSS

Anyway.

MARTIN

Anyway, it was pretty wonderful. And I was getting back in the car, about to get back in the car, all my loot—vegetables and stuff . . . (*change of tone to quiet wonder*) and it was then that I saw her. (*Sees it*) Just . . . just looking at me.

ROSS

Daisy Mae! Blonde hair to her shoulders, big tits in the calico blouse, bare midriff, blonde down at the navel, piece a straw in her teeth . . .

MARTIN

(*Gentle, admonishing smile*) You don't understand.

ROSS

No? No blonde hair? No tits?

MARTIN

No. And there she was, looking at me with those eyes.

ROSS

And it was love.

MARTIN

You don't understand.

ROSS

No? It *wasn't* love?

MARTIN

No. Yes; yes, it was love, but I didn't know it right then. (*To himself*) How could I?

ROSS

Right then it was good old lust, eh? Dick starting to get big in your pants . . .

MARTIN

(*Sad*) You *don't* understand. (*Pause*) I didn't know *what* it was
—what I was feeling. It was . . . it wasn't like anything I'd felt
before; it was . . . so . . . amazing, so . . . extraordinary! There
she was, just looking at me, with those *eyes* of hers, and . . .

ROSS

(*Impatient*) Well, did you *talk* to her?

MARTIN

(*Incredulous laugh*) Did I *what*!?

ROSS

Did you *talk* to her!?

MARTIN

(*Considers it*) Hunh! Yes; yes, I did. I went up to her, to where
she was, and I spoke to her, and she came toward me and . . .
and those eyes, and I touched her face, and . . . (*Abrupt*) I
don't want to talk about it; I can't *talk* about it.

ROSS

All right; let me help you. You're *seeing* her.

MARTIN

(*Sad laugh*) Yes; oh, yes; I'm *seeing* her.

ROSS

You're having an affair with her.

MARTIN

(*Confused*) A what? Having a *what*!?

ROSS

(*Hard*) You're *screwing* her.

MARTIN

(*Sudden vision of it*) Yes; yes; I'm *screwing* her. Oh, Jesus!

ROSS

(*Softer*) And you're in love.

MARTIN

That's it, you see.

ROSS

What is? What do I see?

MARTIN

I *am* seeing her; I *am* having . . . an affair, I guess. No! That's
not the right word. I am . . . (*winces*) screwing her, as you put
it—all of which is . . . beyond even . . . yes, I'm doing all that.

ROSS

(*Prompting*) . . . and you're in love with her.

MARTIN

(*Begins to cry*) Yes! Yes! I am! I'm in love with her. Oh, Jesus!
Oh, Sylvia! Oh, Sylvia!

ROSS

(*After a respectful pause*) I almost dare not ask this, but . . .
who is Sylvia?

MARTIN

I can't tell you!

ROSS

Who else *but* me? You can't tell Stevie, it would . . .

MARTIN

NO!!

ROSS

Then, who is she? Who is Sylvia?

(MARTIN *pauses; goes to wallet, brings out photo, looks at it, hesitates,
then hands it to* ROSS, *not looking as he does so.* ROSS *takes photo, looks at
it, double-takes, begins a huge guffaw, which becomes a coughing*)

MARTIN

(*Shy*) Don't laugh. Please; don't laugh.

ROSS

(*Staring at photo; straightforward*) This is Sylvia.

MARTIN

(*Nods*) Yes.

ROSS

(*Pinning it down*) This is Sylvia . . . who you're fucking.

MARTIN

(*Winces*) Don't say that. (*It just comes out*) Whom.

ROSS

. . . with whom you're having an affair.

MARTIN

(*Soft; nodding*) Yes. (*Pause*) Yes.

ROSS

How long now?

MARTIN

(*Soft*) Six months.

ROSS

Jesus. You *have* to tell Stevie.

MARTIN

I can't! I couldn't do that!

ROSS

You *have* to . . . and if you don't, I will.

MARTIN

(*Begging*) No! Ross! Please!

ROSS

(*Genuine*) You're in very serious trouble.

MARTIN

(*Pause; little boy*) I am?

ROSS

(*Quiet; shaking his head as he looks at the photo*) You sure are, buddy; you sure are.

MARTIN

But, Ross, you don't under . . .

ROSS

(*Huge*) THIS IS A GOAT! YOU'RE HAVING AN AFFAIR WITH A GOAT! YOU'RE FUCKING A GOAT!

MARTIN

(*Long pause; factual*) Yes.

End of Scene One

Scene Two

(*The living room; a day later.* MARTIN, STEVIE, *and* BILLY; STEVIE *holding a letter*)

BILLY

(*To* MARTIN) You're doing *what*?! You're fucking a *goat*?!

MARTIN

(*Indicating* STEVIE, *who is at window, facing out*) Billy! Please!

BILLY

Jesus Christ!

MARTIN

Don't swear.

BILLY

(*Scoffing laugh*) Don't *what*?!

MARTIN

Don't swear; you're too young.

BILLY

(*Considers a moment, then*) FUCK THAT!!

MARTIN

Billy! Your mother!

BILLY

(*Scoffing laugh*) You're fucking a fucking goat and you tell me
not to *swear*?!

MARTIN

You know, your *own* sex life leaves a little to . . .

STEVIE

(*Still at window; ice*) All right, you two!

BILLY

(*To* MARTIN) At least what I do is with . . . persons!

STEVIE

(*Turning into the room*) I said, all right, you two!

BILLY

Goat fucker!

MARTIN

Fucking faggot!

STEVIE

I said, all right!

(*A silence*)

BILLY

(*To* MARTIN; *soft, hurt*) Fucking faggot? You called me a fucking *faggot*?!

MARTIN

(*Gentle; to* BILLY) I'm . . . I'm sorry.

STEVIE

(*Even*) Your father's sorry, Billy.

MARTIN

I'm sorry. (*To get rid of the whole subject*) You're gay, and
that's fine, and I don't give a shit what you put where. (*Thinks
about it*) I don't care one way or the other is what I mean.

BILLY

Yeah! Sure!

STEVIE

(*Cool*) I said your father's sorry for calling you a fucking faggot because he's not that kind of man. He's a decent, liberal,
right-thinking, talented, famous, gentle man (*hard*) who right
now would appear to be fucking a goat; and *I* would like to
talk about *that*, *if* you don't mind. *Or* . . . even if you *do*.

BILLY

(*Nice*) Sure, Mom; I'm sorry; you go right ahead.

MARTIN

(*Sighs*) Oh, dear.

STEVIE

(*Objective*) Let's review Ross's letter, shall we? (*waves it*)

MARTIN

(*Hurt and enraged*) How *could* he!! How could he do such a
thing?!

STEVIE

(*Ice*) How could he—best friend to both of us, a man you
would trust with your wife—no? . . .

MARTIN

. . . sure; sure . . .

STEVIE

How could Ross write me this letter? (*waves it again*)

MARTIN

YES!!

STEVIE

(*Composed; cool; quoting*) ". . . because I love you, Stevie, as
much as I love Martin, because I love you both—respect you,
love you—I can't stay silent at a time of crisis for you both, for
Martin's public image, and your own deeply devoted . . . "

MARTIN

BULLSHIT!

STEVIE

Yes?

MARTIN

Yes!

STEVIE

So; anyhow; let's not pretend he never wrote the letter; let's not pretend I didn't get it in the mail today—nice that: no electronic nonsense—and let us not pretend that I did not read it.

MARTIN

No; no, of course not.

STEVIE

And let us not pretend that Ross does not tell me that you are having an affair with . . . (*looks*) how does he put it? . . . "an affair with a certain Sylvia who, I am mortified to tell you . . ." He does get flowery, doesn't he!

MARTIN

Yes; yes, he does.

STEVIE

"I am mortified to tell you is a goat."

BILLY

Jesus!

STEVIE & MARTIN

Will you be still!!?

BILLY

(*Dramatically cowering*) Hey! Sure! Jesus!

STEVIE

(*Back to business; quoting again*) "You will, of course, be

shocked and greatly distressed . . ." No kidding! Uh . . .
"shocked and greatly distressed to know of this, but I felt it my
obligation to be the one to bear these tidings . . . "

MARTIN

(*Some disbelief*) Tidings?

STEVIE

Yes; "tidings."

MARTIN

Jesus! Of comfort and joy?

STEVIE

" . . . as I'm sure you'd rather hear it all from a dear friend . . ."
As opposed to *what*! The ASPCA?!

MARTIN

(*Woe*) Oh, God; oh, God.

STEVIE

"Doubtless, Martin . . . " Doubtless?

MARTIN

Probably.

STEVIE

" . . . doubtless Martin will tell you all I have not, all I cannot." (*To* MARTIN) What are friends for, eh?

BILLY

(*Really sad*) Oh, Dad!

MARTIN

Poor Dad?

BILLY

What?

MARTIN

Nothing.

STEVIE

(*Level*) So, now you will tell me all that Ross has not, cannot. After you tell me what friends are for, of course.

MARTIN

Oh . . . Stevie . . . (*Starts to move to her*)

STEVIE

(*Abrupt; cold*) Stay away from me; stay there. You smell of goat, you smell of shit, you smell of all I cannot imagine being able to smell. Stay *away* from me!

MARTIN

(*Arms wide; hopeless*) I *love* you!

BILLY

(*Softly*) Jesus.

STEVIE

You *love* me. Let's see if I understand the phrase. You *love* me.

MARTIN

Yes!

STEVIE

But I'm a human being; I have only two breasts; I walk upright; I give milk only on special occasions; I use the toilet. (*Begins to cry*) You love me? I don't understand.

MARTIN

(*More hopeless*) Oh, God!

STEVIE

How can you love me when you love so much less?

MARTIN

(*Even more hopeless*) Oh, God.

BILLY

Fucking a goat?!

MARTIN

(To BILLY; sharp) That does it! Out!

BILLY

(*To* STEVIE; *arms wide*) What did I *say*? I said he was . . .

MARTIN

Enough!

BILLY

For Christ's sake, I . . .

MARTIN

Go to your room!

STEVIE

(*Almost laughing*) Oh, really, Martin!

BILLY

(*Incredulous*) Go to my room?!

MARTIN

Go to your *room*!

BILLY

What am I—eight, or something? Go to my *room*?

STEVIE

You'd better go, Billy. If you stay you might learn something.

MARTIN

(*To* STEVIE) Nicely put.

STEVIE

(*Coldly*) Thanks.

BILLY

(*To* STEVIE) You want me to leave you here with this . . .
this . . . *pervert*?!

STEVIE

(*To help*) Just go to your room, Billy, or go outside, or . . .

MARTIN

. . . or go to one of your public urinals, or one of those death clubs, or . . .

BILLY

KNOCK IT OFF!!

MARTIN

(*Impressed*) Wow!

BILLY

(*Sneering*) You seem to know a lot about all that.

MARTIN

(*Not defensive*) I *read*.

BILLY

Sure. (*To* STEVIE) I'll go if you think it's OK, Ma; I'll go. (*To* MARTIN) But not to your . . . "places." I will probably go to my room, and I'll probably close my door, and I'll probably lie down on my bed, and I'll probably start crying and it'll probably get louder and worse, but you probably won't hear it—either of you—because you'll be too busy killing each other. But I'll be there, and my little eight-year-old heart will for certain be breaking—in twain, as they say.

MARTIN

(*Some awe; no contempt*) Very good; very good.

STEVIE

(*Preoccupied*) Yes; very good, Billy.

BILLY

(*Fleeing; near tears*) Jesus Christ!

STEVIE

(*As he exits*) Billy . . .

MARTIN

(*Quietly*) Let him go. (*Silence; quietly*) Well, now; just you and me.

STEVIE

(*Pause*) Yes.

MARTIN

(*Pause*) I take it you want to talk about it?

STEVIE

(*Awful chuckle*) Oh, God! (*Afterthought*) You *take* it?

MARTIN

Is that a "yes"?

STEVIE

(*Cold; precise*) I was out shopping today—dress gloves, if you want to know. I still wear them—for weddings and things . . .

MARTIN

(*Puzzled*) Who's getting married?

STEVIE

(Huge) SHUT UP!

MARTIN

(*Winces*) Sorry.

STEVIE

(*Normal tone again*) . . . dress gloves, and then to the fish people for shad roe—it's just come in—and then back home, and you were gone and I heard Billy's music up in his room and there was the mail. You'd gone out before it came—not that it would have mattered: we don't read each other's.

MARTIN

Would that we did.

STEVIE

Oh? I would have found out sooner or later. And there was Ross's letter. "Ross? Writing to me? Whatever for!"

MARTIN

(*Softly*) Oh, God.

STEVIE

. . . and I was standing in the pantry. I'd put the roe away and had left the kitchen and was moving to the dining room on my way to the stairs when I began to read it.

MARTIN

Ross shouldn't have done this. He *knows* he shouldn't have done . . .

STEVIE

(*Reading; steady, almost amused*) "Dearest Stevie . . . "

MARTIN

Oh, God.

STEVIE

"This is the hardest letter I've ever had to write."

MARTIN

Sure!

STEVIE

You doubt it? ". . . the hardest letter I've ever had to write, and to my dearest friends. But because I love you, Stevie, as much as I love Martin, because I love you both—respect you, love you—I can't stay silent at a time of crisis for you both, for Martin's public image and your own deeply devoted . . ."

MARTIN

As I said, bullshit.

STEVIE

. . . "self. I must put it baldly, for hinting would only put off

the inevitable. Martin—and he told me this himself" . . .
(*aside*) I would have liked to have been listening to *that* conversation!

MARTIN

No you wouldn't.

STEVIE

(*Reading again*) "Martin is having an affair with a certain
Sylvia . . . " (*To* MARTIN) Oh, God, I thought; at least it's
someone I don't know; at least it's not Ross's first wife, the one
I thought you might if you were going to . . .

MARTIN

(*Surprise*) Rebecca?

STEVIE

Yes, or maybe your new assistant . . .

MARTIN

(*Bewildered*) Who? Ted Ryan?

STEVIE

No; the *other* one—the one with the hooters.

MARTIN

Oh; Lucy something.

STEVIE

Yes: Lucy "something." You men are the end. Where was I?
(*reads again*) . . . "an affair with a certain Sylvia who, I am
mortified to tell you . . . is a goat. You will, of course, be
shocked and greatly disturbed to know of this, but I felt it my
obligation to be the one to bear these tidings, as I'm sure
you'd rather hear it from a dear friend. Doubtless, Martin . . ."
Doubtless?

MARTIN

(*Shrugs*) Sounds right.

STEVIE

"Doubtless, Martin will tell you all I have not . . . all I cannot. With profound affection for you both, Ross." (*Pause*) Well.

MARTIN

Yes. "Well."

STEVIE

(*Not eager; dogged*) We will now discuss it.

MARTIN

(*Heavy sigh*) Of course, though you won't understand.

STEVIE

Oh? Do you know what I thought—what I thought after I'd read the letter, right to the end?

MARTIN

No, I don't want to know . . . or guess.

STEVIE

Well, I laughed, of course: a grim joke but an awfully funny one. "That Ross, I tell you, that Ross! You go too far, Ross. It's funny . . . in its . . . awful way, but it's way overboard, Ross!" So, I shook my head and laughed—at the awfulness of it, the absurdity, the awfulness; some things are so awful you have to laugh—and then I listened to myself laughing, and I began to wonder why I *was*—*laughing*. "It's not funny when you come right down to it, Ross" Why *was* I laughing? And just like that (*snaps her fingers*) I stopped; I stopped laughing. I realized— probably in the way if you suddenly fell off a building—oh, shit! I've fallen off a building and I'm going to die; I'm going to go splat on the sidewalk; like *that*—that it wasn't a joke at all; it was awful and absurd, but it wasn't a joke. And every- thing tied in—Ross coming here to interview you yesterday, the funny smell, the Noel Coward bit we did about you having an affair, and with a goat. You said it right out and I laughed. You told me! You came right out and fucking *told* me, and I laughed, and I made jokes about going to the feed store, and I *laughed*. I fucking laughed! Until it stopped; until the laughter stopped. Until it all came together—Ross's letter and all the rest: that odd smell . . . the mistress's perfume on you. And so I knew.

MARTIN

Stevie, I'm so . . .

STEVIE

Shut up. And so I knew. And next, of course, came believing it. Knowing it—knowing it's true is one thing, but *believing* what you *know* . . . well, there's the tough part. We all prepare for jolts along the way, disturbances of the peace, the lies, the evasions, the infidelities—*if* they happen. (*Very off-hand*) I've never had an affair, by the way, all our years together; not even with a cat, or . . . *any*thing.

MARTIN

Oh, Stevie . . .

STEVIE

We prepare for . . . things, for lessenings, even; inevitable . . . lessenings, and we think we can handle everything, whatever comes along, but we don't know, *do* we! (*Right at* MARTIN) *Do* we!

MARTIN

(*Bereaved*) No; no, we don't.

STEVIE

Fucking *right* we don't! (*Didactic*) Something can happen that's outside the rules, that doesn't relate to The Way the Game Is Played. Death before you're ready to even think about it—that's part of the game. A stroke that leaves you sitting looking at an eggplant the week before had been your husband—that's another. Emotional disengagement, gradual, so gradual you don't know it's happening, or sudden—not very often, but occasionally—that's another. You've read about spouses—God! I hate that word!—"spouses" who all of a sudden start wearing dresses—yours, or their own collection —wives gone dyke . . . but if there's one thing you *don't* put on your plate, no matter how exotic your tastes may be is . . . bestiality.

MARTIN

Don't! You don't understand.

STEVIE

The fucking of animals! No, that's one thing you haven't thought about, one thing you've overlooked as a byway on the road of life, as the old soap has it. "Well, I wonder when he'll start cruising livestock. I must ask Mother whether Dad did it and how *she* handled it." No, that's the one thing you haven't thought about—nor could you conceive of. (*Pause; grimly cheerful*) So! How was *your* day?

MARTIN

(*Pause; attempting the casual*) Well . . . I had a good day at the office. Made the design for The World City even larger than . . .

STEVIE

(*Fixed smile*) Oh, good!

MARTIN

. . . and then I stopped by the haberdasher . . .

STEVIE

(*Pretending to puzzle*) Ha-ber-dash-er. That's someone who makes haberdash?

MARTIN

Haber, I think. Dash is part of doing it.

STEVIE

Ah! *Then* what?

MARTIN

Hm? Well, then I drove back home, and . . .

STEVIE

What! You didn't stop by to see your ladyfriend? Get a lick in?

MARTIN

She's in the country. Please, Stevie . . . *don't*!

STEVIE
(*Feigned wonder*) She's in the *country*!

MARTIN
I keep her there.

STEVIE
Where!?

MARTIN
Please! Don't!

STEVIE
Martin, did you ever think you'd come back from your splendid life, walk into your living room and find you had no life left?

MARTIN
Not specifically; no. (*Looks down*)

STEVIE
I think we'd better talk about this. If I'm going to kill you I need to know exactly why—all the details.

MARTIN
(*Shy*) You really want to?

STEVIE
What? Kill you?

MARTIN
No; learn about it.

STEVIE
(*Big*) No! I *don't* really want to! (*Normal tone again*) I want the whole day to rewind—start over. I want the reel to reverse: to see the mail on the hall table where Billy's left it, then *not* see it because I haven't opened the door yet—not having gotten the fish yet because I haven't bought the gloves yet because I haven't left the house yet because I haven't gotten

out of our bed because I haven't *waked* UP YET!! (*Quieter*)
But . . . since I can't reverse time . . . yes, I *do* want to know.
I'm reeling with it. (*Pleading*) Make me not *believe* it! Please,
make me *not believe* it.

MARTIN

(*Pause*) Why aren't you crying?

STEVIE

Because this is too serious. Do goats cry, by the way?

MARTIN

I . . . I don't know. I haven't . . .

STEVIE

. . . made her cry yet!? What's the *matter* with you?!

MARTIN

(*Begging*) Stevie . . .

STEVIE

(*As if to someone else*) He can't even make a *goat* cry. What
good is he? His son's probably weeping as we speak. That was
pretty awful what you said to him, Martin, pretty awful. His
son's probably lying on his bed, tears flowing; his wife *would*
be crying (*harder*) except she can't be that weak right now.
And you can't even make a goat cry?! Jeez!

MARTIN

(*Dogmatic*) I didn't say I *couldn't*; I said I *haven't*.

STEVIE

Well, the goats of this world must be very happy. Oh, you kid!

MARTIN

(*Starting to leave*) I can't *have* this conversation. I can't listen
to you when you're . . .

STEVIE

(*Blocking him*) You *stay* where you *are*! You will *have* this
conversation, and with *me* and right *now*!

MARTIN

(*Retreating; sighing*) Where shall I start?

STEVIE

(*A threat*) Right at the beginning! (*Afterthought*) Why do you
call her Sylvia, by the way? Did she have a tag, or something?
Or, was it more: Who is Sylvia,
                      Fair is she
                      That all our goats commend her . . .

MARTIN

(*Trying to be rational*) No, it just seemed right. Very good, by
the way.

STEVIE

Thank you. You saw this . . . *thing* . . . this goat, and you said
to yourself "This is Sylvia." Or did you talk to it: "Hello,
Sylvia." How the hell did you know it was a she—was a
female? Bag of nipples dragging in the dung? Or, isn't this
your first?!

MARTIN

(*Very quiet*) She is my first; she is my only. But you don't understand. You . . .

STEVIE

(*Contemptuous*) Awww; I'm trying not to throw up.

MARTIN

Well, if that's the way you . . .

STEVIE

No!! Tell me.

MARTIN

(*Sighs*) All right. As I said to Ross . . .

STEVIE

(*Broad parody*) "As I said to Ross . . . " *NO*! Not "As I said to
Ross." To *me*! As you say to *me*!

MARTIN

(*Annoyed*) In any event . . .

STEVIE

Not "in any event!" No! *This* event!

MARTIN

(Won't let it go) As I said to Ross . . .

STEVIE

(*Impatient acquiescence*) *Very* well; as you said to Ross.

MARTIN

Thank you. As I said to Ross, I'd gone to the country . . . to find the place we wanted, our . . . country *place*.

STEVIE

(*Fact*) You went out a lot.

MARTIN

Well, if you're after Utopia . . . (*Shrugs*)

STEVIE

Sure.

MARTIN

. . . unless you're one of those people finds it right off: "That's it; that's the place." Unless you're one of those, you've got to search; look around. Close enough in to make it practical for our country needs. No more than an hour or so from . . .

STEVIE

(*Scoffing*) Our "country needs"?

MARTIN

You're the one who said it. Verdancy: flowers and green leaves against steel and stone. OK?

STEVIE

(*Shrugs*) OK. (*Angry*) And it's lovely. Now get to the *goat*!

MARTIN

I'm *getting* there. I'm *getting* to her.

STEVIE

Stop calling it *her*!

MARTIN

(*Defending*) *That* is what she *is*! It is a *she*! *She* is a *she*!

STEVIE

(*Pathetic sneer*) I suppose I should be grateful it wasn't a *male*, *isn't* a male goat.

MARTIN

Funny you should ask—as they say. There was a place I went to . . .

STEVIE

Oh?

MARTIN

Well, when I realized something was wrong. I mean, when I realized people would *think* something was wrong, that what I was doing wasn't . . .

STEVIE

(*Dispassionate*) I *am* going to kill you.

MARTIN

(*Preoccupied*) Yes; probably. It was a therapy place, a place people went to . . . to talk about it, about what they were doing . . . and with whom.

STEVIE

What! Not *whom*! *What*! With *what*!

MARTIN

(*Sharp*) Whatever! A place! Please! Let me finish this! (STEVIE *is silent*) A place to talk about it; like AA, like Alcoholics Anonymous.

STEVIE

(*Sneers*) Goat-fuckers Anonymous?

MARTIN

(*Oddly shocked*) Please! (STEVIE *hoots. Quieter*) Please?

STEVIE

Sorry. Destroy me.

MARTIN

It had no cute name; no AA; no . . . no nothing. Just . . . a place.

STEVIE

How did you find it?

MARTIN

Online.

STEVIE

(*Toneless*) Of course.

MARTIN

I went there . . . and there were—what?—ten of us . . . a group leader, of course.

STEVIE

What was *he* fucking? *Who*; sorry.

MARTIN

He was cured, he said—odd phrase. Was off it.

STEVIE

(*Very calm*) Very well. What *had* he been fucking?

MARTIN

(*Matter of fact*) A pig. A young pig.

(STEVIE *rises, finds a big ceramic table plate, smashes it, resits, or whatever*)

STEVIE

(*Without emotion*) Go on.

MARTIN

(*Indicates*) Is there going to be a lot of that?

STEVIE

Probably.

MARTIN

You don't want Billy down here; some things . . .

STEVIE

(*Steaming*) Some things are . . . *what*?! Private? Sacred?
Husband telling wifey about a very peculiar therapy session?
A *pig*?!

MARTIN

(*A little embarrassed*) A small one, he said.

STEVIE

Jesus!

(BILLY *rushes in from the hall*)

BILLY

You two OK?

MARTIN

Yes-we're-fine-go-away-Billy.

BILLY

Who's throwing things?

STEVIE

I am; your mother is throwing things.

BILLY

Is there going to be more?

STEVIE

I imagine so.

BILLY

(*Retrieving a small vase*) I gave you this one; I think I'll take it upstairs.

STEVIE

(*As* BILLY *turns to go*) I would have noticed, Billy.

BILLY

(*Shaking his head*) Sure. You guys hold it down. (*Exits*)

STEVIE

(*After him*) I *would* have. (*Uncertain*) I *think* I would have.

MARTIN

(*Pause*) So, anyway; it was this place.

STEVIE

(*Reconcentrating*) A pig? Really?

MARTIN

Well, everyone had . . . *you* know . . .

STEVIE

 . . . some*one*, or some*thing*.

MARTIN

Yes.

STEVIE

(*Lightbulb*) And was Clarissa Atherton there?

MARTIN

Who? Yes! That's where I got the card, and . . .

STEVIE

And what is *she* fucking? *Who*?

MARTIN

(*Matter of fact*) A dog, I think.
(STEVIE *finds a vase, crashes it to the floor*)

STEVIE

A dog you *think*.

MARTIN

Why would she lie? Why would anyone there lie?

STEVIE

Damned if *I* know.

MARTIN

(*Sighs*) And so I went there, and . . .

STEVIE

(*There is chaos behind the civility, of course*) Did you all take
your . . . friends with you—your pigs, your dogs, your goats,
your . . .

MARTIN

No. We weren't there to talk about *them*; we were there about
ourselves, our . . . our problems, as they called them.

STEVIE

The livestock was all happy, you mean.

MARTIN

Well, no; there was this one . . . goose, I think it was . . .
(STEVIE *finds a vase, crashes it to the floor*) Shall we go
outside?

STEVIE

(*Hands on hips*) Get *on* with it.

MARTIN

(*So calm*) All right; there was this one goose . . .

STEVIE

Not geese! *Not* pigs! *Not* dogs! *Goats*! The subject is *goats*!

MARTIN

The subject is *a* goat; the subject is Sylvia. (*He sees* STEVIE *looking for something to throw*) No! Don't; please! Just listen! Sit and listen!

STEVIE

(*Has a small bowl in her hands; sits*) All right. I'm listening.

MARTIN

I said, most of the people there were having problems, were . . . ashamed, or—what is the word?—conflicted . . . were . . . needed to talk about it while . . . while I went there, I guess, to find out why they were all there.

STEVIE

(*As if the language were unfamiliar*) Pardon?

MARTIN

I didn't understand why they were there—why they were all so . . . unhappy; what was wrong with . . . with . . . being in love . . . like that. (STEVIE *gently separates hands, letting bowl fall between her legs, break*) There's so much I have to explain.

STEVIE

(*Deep, quiet irony*) Oh?

MARTIN

(*Rises, moves a little away*) You must promise to be still. Sit there and please listen, and then maybe when I've finished you . . . just listen; please.

STEVIE

(*Sad smile*) How could I not?

MARTIN

I went there . . . because I couldn't come to *you* with it.

STEVIE

Oh?

MARTIN

Well . . . *think* about it.

STEVIE

(*Does*) I suppose you're right.

MARTIN

And most of them had a problem, had a long history. The man with the pig was a farmboy, and he and his brothers, when they were kids, just . . . *did* it . . . *naturally*; it was what they did . . . with the pigs. (*Knits brow*) Or piglets, perhaps; that wasn't clear.

STEVIE

Naturally; of course.

MARTIN

Are you agreeing?

STEVIE

No. Just get on with it.

MARTIN

It was what they did. Maybe it was better than . . .

STEVIE

. . . than with each other, or their sisters, or their grand-mothers? You've got to be kidding!

MARTIN

No one got hurt.

STEVIE

HUNH!!

MARTIN

We'll talk about that.

STEVIE

You *bet* we will!

MARTIN

(*Sighs*) Most of them had a reason, the man with the pig more a matter of . . . habit than anything else, I guess . . . comfort, familiarity.

STEVIE

(*Eyes heavenward*) Jesus!

MARTIN

Though he was off it . . . "cured," as he put it, which I found odd.

STEVIE

Of course.

MARTIN

I mean . . . if he was happy . . .

(STEVIE *knocks over the small side table where she is sitting, never taking her eyes off* MARTIN)

STEVIE

(*Ironic*) Ooops!

MARTIN

When he was doing it, I mean. Must you? Though I suppose he wasn't . . . no longer was happy.

STEVIE

(*Feigned surprise*) You mean you didn't *ask* him?

MARTIN

No; no, I didn't. The lady with the German Shepherd . . .

STEVIE

Clarissa?

MARTIN

No; another one. The lady with the Shepherd, it turned out

she had been raped by her father *and* her brother when she was twelve, or so . . . continually raped, one watching the other, she told us . . .

STEVIE

. . . and so she took up with a *dog*?!

MARTIN

(*No opinion*) Yes; it would seem. The man with the goose was . . . hideously ugly—I could barely look at him—and I suppose he thought he could never . . . *you* know.

STEVIE

(*Cool*) Do I?

MARTIN

Try and imagine.

STEVIE

(*Calm; sad*) I doubt I can.

MARTIN

Try: so ugly, no woman—no *man*—would even *think* of . . . "doing it" with you—*ever*.

STEVIE

One in the hand, et cetera. But . . . a goose!?

MARTIN

(*Sad smile*) Not everyone is satisfied that way . . . one in the hand. No matter. And *I* was unhappy there, for *they* were all unhappy.

STEVIE

My goodness.

MARTIN

And I didn't know why.

STEVIE

(*Considers it*) Really? I think we've hit upon why I'm going to kill you.

MARTIN

(*Onward*) There's something else I want you to understand.

STEVIE

(*Sarcasm*) Oh? Something else?

MARTIN

It's something I told Ross.

STEVIE

Not him again.

MARTIN

He *is* my best friend.

STEVIE

(*Actress-y*) Oh? And I thought *I* was!

MARTIN

(*Undeterred; calm*) I told him that in all our time together —yours and mine—all our marriage—I've never been unfaithful.

STEVIE

(*A beat; fake astonishment*) *Hunh*!!

MARTIN

(*Onward*) Never in all our years. Oh, early on, one of your friends would grope me in the kitchen at a party, or . . .

STEVIE

I love my friends; they have taste.

MARTIN

Never unfaithful; never once. I've never even wanted to. We're so good together, you and I.

STEVIE

A perfect fit, eh?

MARTIN

(*Sincere*) Yes!

STEVIE

You'd never imagine that a marriage could be so perfect.

MARTIN

Yes! I mean *no*; I *hadn't*.

STEVIE

(*Advertisement*) Great sex, good cook, even does windows.

MARTIN

Be serious!

STEVIE

No! It's too serious for that. (*Afterthought*) Fuck you, by the way.

MARTIN

Never once! People looked at me, said "What's the matter with you?!" "Don't you have any . . . you know, lust?" And "Sure," I said, "I've got plenty. All for Stevie."

STEVIE

(*Shakes her head; sing-song*) La-di-da; la-di-fuckin'-da!

MARTIN

(*Rage*) Listen to me!

STEVIE

(*Army drill*) Yes, Sir! (*Softer*) Yes, Sir.

MARTIN

All the men I knew were "having affairs" . . . *see*ing other women, and laughing about it—at the club, on the train. I felt . . . well, I almost felt like a misfit. "What's the matter with you, Martin!? You mean you're only doing it with your wife!? What kind of man *are* you?!"

STEVIE

You men *must* be fun together.

MARTIN

Odd man out. I only wanted *you*.

STEVIE

(*Pause; quietly*) And *I* have something to tell *you*.

MARTIN

(*Anticipating, with dread*) Oh, no! Don't tell me that you've been with . . .

STEVIE

(*Hands up; shakes her head*) Hush. In all our marriage I've never even wanted anyone but you.

MARTIN

(*Deeply sad*) Oh, Stevie.

STEVIE

My mother told me—we really *were* good friends; I'm sorry you never knew her.

MARTIN

I am, too.

STEVIE

We talked together like sisters, by God; we talked the night away, two "girls" talking; we were that good friends, but she sure knew how to be a "parent" when she needed to, when she wanted to keep me very . . . level. And she said to me—I never told you this—"Be sure you marry someone you're in love with—deeply and wholly in love with—but be careful who you fall in love with, because you might marry him." (MARTIN *chuckles, quietly, ruefully*) "Your father and I have the best marriage anyone could possibly have," she said to me, over and over. "Be sure you do, too."

MARTIN

Stevie, I . . .

STEVIE

"Be careful who you marry," she said to me. And I *was*. I *fell* in love with you? No . . . I rose into love with you and have—what—*cherished*? you, all these years, been proud of all you've done, been happy with our . . . funny son, been . . . well, happy. I guess that's the word. No, I don't guess; I *know*. (*Begins to cry*) I've been happy. (*More*) Look at me, Mother; I've married the man I loved (*more*) and I've been . . . so . . . happy.

MARTIN

(*Moves to her; touches her*) Oh, Stevie . . .

STEVIE

(*Huge; swipes objects off the coffee table*) GET YOUR GOAT-FUCKING HANDS OFF ME!!! (*Retreats to wall, arms wide, sobbing greatly*)

MARTIN

(*Reacts as if he's touched a hot stove*) All right! No more!

STEVIE

Yes! *More*! Finish it! Vomit it all up! Puke it out all over me. I'll never be less ready. So . . . *do* it! *DO* IT!! I've laid it all out for you; I'm naked on the table; take all your knives! Cut me! Scar me forever!

MARTIN

(*Thinks a moment*) Before or *after* I vomit on you? (*Gently; hands up to appease*) Sorry; sorry.

STEVIE

(*A shaking voice*) Women in deep woe often mix their metaphors.

MARTIN

(*Pacifying*) Yes; yes.

STEVIE

Get *on* with it! (*Afterthought*) Very good, by the way.

MARTIN

(*Rue*) Thanks.

STEVIE

. . . and hopelessly inappropriate.

MARTIN

Yes; sorry.

STEVIE

(*Casually overturns a chair*) Get on with it, I said.

MARTIN

Are you going to do that with *all* the furniture?

STEVIE

(*Looks around*) I think so. You may have to help me with some of it.

MARTIN

Truce! Truce!

STEVIE

(*Takes a painting, breaks it over something*) NO! NO TRUCE! *All* of it! Now!

MARTIN

That was my mother's painting.

STEVIE

It still is! (*Prompting*) You found us our lovely country place.

MARTIN

(*Girds*) And the day I found it—I called you. You remember: I told you I'd put a hold on it.

STEVIE

I'll never forget.

MARTIN

And I was driving out of the town, back to the highway, and I stopped at the top of a hill . . .

STEVIE

Crest.

MARTIN

What!? Who *are* you!?

STEVIE

You stopped at the crest of a hill—on it, actually.

MARTIN

Yes. And I stopped, and the view was . . . wonderful. Not spectacular, but wonderful—fall, the leaves turning . . .

STEVIE

(*Staring at him*) A regular bucolic.

MARTIN

Yes; a regular bucolic. I stopped and got us things—vegetables and things. *You* remember.

STEVIE

(*Denial*) No; I don't.

MARTIN

(*Realizing, going on*) No matter. And it was then that I saw her.

STEVIE

(*Grotesque incomprehension*) *Who*!?

MARTIN

(*Deeply sad*) Oh, Stevie . . .

STEVIE

(*Heavy irony*) *Who*!? *Who* could you have seen!?

MARTIN

(*Dogged*) I'm going on with this. You asked. I'm going to get it all out.

STEVIE

(*Eyes hard on him*) Serves *me* right, I guess.

MARTIN

And I closed the trunk of the car, with all that I'd gotten— (*pause*) . . . and it was then that I saw her. And she was looking at me with . . . with those eyes.

STEVIE

(*Staring at him*) Oh, those eyes! (*Afterthought*) *THEM* eyes!

MARTIN

(*Slow; deliberate*) And what I felt was . . . it was unlike anything I'd ever felt before. It was so . . . amazing. There she was.

STEVIE

(*Grotesque enthusiasm*) Who!? Who!?

MARTIN

Don't. She was looking at me with those eyes of hers and . . . I melted, I think. I think that's what I did: I melted.

STEVIE

(*Hideous enthusiasm*) You melted!!

MARTIN

(*Waves her off*) I'd never seen such an expression. It was pure . . . and trusting and . . . and innocent; so . . . so guileless.

STEVIE

(*Sardonic echo*) Guileless; innocent; pure. You've never seen children, or anything? You never saw Billy when he was a kid?

MARTIN

(*Pleading*) Of course I did. Don't *mock* me.

STEVIE
(*Shooting harsh chuckle*) Don't mock *me*.

MARTIN
I . . . I went over to where she was—to the fence where she was, and I knelt there, eye level . . .

STEVIE
(*Quiet loathing*) *Goat* level.

MARTIN
(*Angry; didactic*) I will *finish* this! You *asked* for it, and you're going to *get* it! So . . . shut your tragic mouth! (STEVIE *does a sharp intake of breath, puts her fingers over her mouth*) All right. Listen to me. It was as if an alien came out of whatever it was, and it . . . took me with it, and it was . . . an ecstasy and a purity, and a . . . love of a . . . (*dogmatic*) un-i-mag-in-able kind, and it relates to nothing *whatever*, to nothing that can be *related* to! Don't you see!? Don't you see the . . . don't you see the "thing" that happened to me? What nobody understands? Why I can't feel what I'm supposed to!? Because it relates to nothing? It can't have happened! It did, but it *can't* have! (STEVIE *shakes her head*) What are you doing?

STEVIE
(*Removes fingers*) Being tragic. I bet a psychiatrist would love all this.

MARTIN
I knelt there, eye level, and there was a . . . a what!? . . . an understanding so intense, so natural . . .

STEVIE
There are some things you *can* remember, eh?

MARTIN
(*Closes his eyes, reopens them*) . . . an understanding so . . .

STEVIE
(*Awful, high-pitched little voice*) I can't remember why I come into rooms, where I put the thing for the razor . . .

MARTIN

(*Refusing to be drawn in*) . . . an understanding so natural, so intense that I will *never* forget it, as intense as the night you and I finally came at the same time. What was it . . . a month after we began? (*Where is she, emotionally?*) Stevie? It wasn't happening . . . but it *was*!

STEVIE

(*Shaking her head; oddly objective*) How *much* do you hate me?

MARTIN

(*Hopeless*) I *love* you. (*Pause*) And I love *her*. (*Pause*) And there it is.

(STEVIE *howls three times, slowly, deliberately; a combination of rage and hurt*)

STEVIE

(*Then; calmly*) Go on.

MARTIN

(*Apologetic*) I have to do it.

STEVIE

Yes? (MARTIN *nods*) Right.

MARTIN

(*Starting again*) And there was a connection there—a communication—that, well . . . an epiphany, I guess comes closest, and I knew what was going to happen.

STEVIE

(*Mildly interested in the fact*) I think I'm going to be sick.

MARTIN

Please don't. (*Back to it*) Epiphany! And when it happens there's no retreating, no holding back. I put my hands through the wires of the fence and she came toward me, slipped her face between my hands, brought her nose to mine at the wires and . . . and nuzzled.

STEVIE

I am a grown woman; a grown married woman. (*As if she's never heard the word before*) Nuzzled; nuzzled.

MARTIN

Her breath . . . her breath was . . . so sweet, warm and . . . (*Hears something; stops*)

STEVIE

Go on. Tell the grown-up married woman . . .

MARTIN

(*Warning hand up*) I hear Billy.

(BILLY *enters*)

BILLY

Are you hitting her!? (*Sees the carnage*) What the fuck!?

STEVIE

We're redecorating, honey. No, he's not, by the way—hitting me. I'm hitting myself.

BILLY

(*Near tears*) I hear you two! I'm up there and I *hear* you! STOP IT! JESUS GOD, STOP IT!!

MARTIN

(*Gentle*) We will, Billy; we're not quite done.

STEVIE

Go away, Billy. Go out and play.

BILLY

Go out and . . . ?

STEVIE

(*Harder*) Leave the house! Leave us alone!

BILLY

But . . .

MARTIN

(*Calm*) Do what your Mother says. "Go out and play." Make mudpies; climb a tree . . .

BILLY

(*A finger in* MARTIN's *face*) If I come back and find you've hurt her, I'll . . . I'll . . . (BILLY *lunges at* MARTIN, *shoves him, recoils.* MARTIN *steps forward, stops.* BILLY *sobs, runs from the room. We hear the front door slam*)

STEVIE

(*After*) Mudpies?

MARTIN

Well . . . whatever.

STEVIE

(*Calm*) What *will* you do if he comes back and finds you've hurt me? . . . *when* he comes back and finds you've hurt me?

MARTIN

(*Absorbed in something*) What?

STEVIE

(*Smiles*) Down from the trees, hands all muddy? (*Sad*) Nothing. (*Cold*) You were in the middle of your Epiphany.

MARTIN

(*Sighs*) Yes.

STEVIE

(*Sad*) God, I wish you were stupid.

MARTIN

(*He, too*) Yes; I wish *you* were stupid, too.

STEVIE

(*Pause; businesslike*) Epiphany!

MARTIN

Yes. It was at that moment that I realized . . .

STEVIE

. . . that you and the fucking goat were destined for one another!

MARTIN

. . . that she and I were . . . (*Softly; embarrassed*) that she and
I were going to go to bed together.

STEVIE

To stall together! To hay! *Not* to bed!

MARTIN

(*Sits*) Whatever. That what could not happen was *going* to.
That we wanted each other very much, that I had to have her,
that I . . . (STEVIE *screams—a deep-throated rage—and lunges
at* MARTIN. *He rises, grabs her wrists and shoves her into a
chair. She attempts to get up, but he shoves her back again*)
Now stop it! Let me finish!

STEVIE

You'll be fucking Billy next.

MARTIN

(*Ice*) He's not my type.

STEVIE

(*Rising again. Rage*) He's not your type!? He's not your fucking type!?

MARTIN

No; he's not. (*She is about to strike him*) *You're* my type.
(*The shock of this stays her gesture; we see her confusion*)
You're my type.

STEVIE

(*Stands where she is; hard*) Thank you!

MARTIN

You're welcome. (*A gesture*) Oh, Stevie, I . . .

STEVIE

I'm your type and so is she; so is the goat. (*Harder*) So long as it's female, eh? So long as it's got a cunt it's all right with you!

MARTIN

(*Huge*) A SOUL!! Don't you know the difference!? Not a cunt, a soul!

STEVIE

(*After a little; tears again*) You can't fuck a soul.

MARTIN

No; and it isn't about fucking.

STEVIE

YES!!

MARTIN

(*As gentle as possible*) No; no, Stevie, it isn't.

STEVIE

(*Pause; then, even more sure*) Yes! It is about fucking! It is about you being an animal!

MARTIN

(*Thinks a moment; quietly*) I thought I was.

STEVIE

(*Contempt*) Hunh!

MARTIN

I thought I was; I thought we *all* were . . . animals.

STEVIE

(*Cold rage*) We stay with our own kind!

MARTIN

(*Gentle; rational*) Oh, we fall in love with *many* other creatures . . . dogs and cats, and . . .

STEVIE

We don't *fuck* them! You're a monster!

MARTIN

(*Pinning it down*) I am a deeply troubled, greatly divided . . .

STEVIE

(No quarter) *Animal* fucker!

MARTIN

Sylvia and I . . .

STEVIE

(*Hideous*) You're going to tell me she *wants* you.

MARTIN

(*Simply put*) Yes.

STEVIE

What does she do—back into you making awful little bleating sounds?

MARTIN

That's sheep.

STEVIE

Whatever!! *Presented* herself? Down on her forelegs, her head turned, her eyes on you, her . . .

MARTIN

Stop it! I won't go into the specifics of our sex with you!

STEVIE

(*Contempt*) *Thank* you! You take advantage of this . . . creature!? You . . . *rape* this . . . animal and convince yourself that it has to do with *love*!?

MARTIN

(*Helpless*) I love her . . . and she loves me, and . . .

STEVIE

(*A huge animal sound: rage; sweeps the bookcase of whatever is on it, or overturns a piece of furniture. Silence; then starting quietly, building*) Now, you listen to me. I have listened to you. I have heard you tell me how much you love me, how you've never even wanted another woman, how we have been a more perfect marriage than chance would even *allow*. We're both too bright for *most* of the shit. We see the deep and awful humor of things go over the heads of most people; we see what's hideously wrong in what most people accept as normal; we have both the joys and the sorrows of all that. We have a straight line through life, right all the way to dying, but that's OK because it's a good line . . . so long as we don't screw up.

MARTIN

I know; I know.

STEVIE

(*Don't interrupt me!*) Shut up; so long as we don't screw up. (*Points at him*) And *you've* screwed *up*!

MARTIN

Stevie, I . . .

STEVIE

I said, shut up. Do you know *how* you've done it? How you've screwed up?

MARTIN

(*Mumbled*) Because I was at the vegetable stand one day, and I looked over to my right and I saw . . .

STEVIE

(*Hard and slow*) Because you've broken something and it can't be fixed!

MARTIN

Stevie . . .

STEVIE

Fall out of love with me? Fine! No, not fine, but that can be fixed . . . time . . . whatever! But tell me you love me and an animal—both of us!—equally? The same way? That you go from my bed—*our* bed . . . (*aside-ish*) it's amazing, you know, how good we are, still, how we please each other *and* ourselves so . . . fully, so . . . fresh each time . . . (*aside over*) . . . you go from our bed, wash your dick, get in your car and go to her, and do with her what I cannot imagine myself imagining? Or—worse! . . . that you've come *from* her, to *my* bed!? To *our* bed!? . . . and you do with me what I *can* imagine . . . love . . . *want* you for!?

MARTIN

(*Deep sadness*) Oh, Stevie . . .

STEVIE

(*Not listening*) That you can do these two things . . . and not understand how it . . . SHATTERS THE GLASS!!?? How it cannot be dealt with—how stop and forgiveness have nothing to do with it? and how I am destroyed? How *you* are? How I cannot admit it though I *know* it!? How I cannot deny it because I cannot *admit* it!? Cannot admit it, because it is outside of denying!?

MARTIN

Stevie, I . . . I promise you, I'll stop; I'll . . .

STEVIE

How stopping has nothing to do with having started?! How nothing has anything to do with anything!? (*Tears—if there—stop*) You have brought me down, you goat-fucker; you love of my life! You have brought me down to *nothing*! (*Accusatory finger right at him*) You have brought me down, and, Christ!, I'll bring you down with me!

(*Brief pause; she turns on her heel, exits. We hear the front door slam.*)

MARTIN

(*After she leaves; after he hears the door; little boy*) Stevie? (*Pause*) Stevie?

End of Scene Two

Scene Three

(*An hour or so later.* MARTIN *is sitting in the ruins. Maybe he is examining a broken piece of something. The room is as it was at the end of Scene Two. The front door slams;* BILLY *enters;* MARTIN *rises and stands in the middle of the room.*)

BILLY
(*Looking around*) Wow!

MARTIN
(*Realizing* BILLY *is there*) Yes; wow.

BILLY
(*Seemingly casual*) You guys really had it out, hunh.

MARTIN
(*Subdued; almost laughing*) *Oh*, yes.

BILLY
Where is she?

MARTIN
Hm? Who?

BILLY

(*Not friendly; overly articulated*) My mother. Where is my mother?

MARTIN

(*Mocking*) Where is "my mother"? Not "Mother—where's Mother?" Not that, but . . . "Where is my mother?"

BILLY

(*Anger rising*) Whatever! Where *is* she? Where is *my mother*?

MARTIN

(*Arms out; helplessly*) I . . . I . . .

BILLY

(*Angrier*) Where *is* she?! What did you do . . . kill her?

MARTIN

(*Softly*) Yes; I think so.

BILLY

(*Dropping something he has picked up*) What!!?

MARTIN

(*Quietly, with a restraining hand*) Stop. No. No, I did not kill her—of *course* not—but I think I might as well have. I think we've killed each other.

BILLY

(*Driving*) Where *is* she!?

MARTIN

(*Simply*) I don't know.

BILLY

What do you mean you don't . . .

MARTIN

(*Loud*) She left!

BILLY

What do you mean she left? Where . . .

MARTIN

(*Snappish*) Stop asking me what I mean! (*Quieter*) She said
what she wanted to say; she finished . . . and she left. She
slammed the front door and left. I assume she drove somewhere.

BILLY

Yeah, the wagon's gone. (*Harder*) Where *is* she!?

MARTIN

(*Loud*) She *left!* I don't know where she *is!* It's English! "She
left." It's English. No, I did not kill her, yes, I think I did, I think
we killed each other. That's English, too: one of your courses!

BILLY

(*Is his rage close to tears? Probably*) I know who you *are*. I
know you're my father. I know who you are, and I know who
you're supposed to be, but . . .

MARTIN

You, too?

BILLY

Hunh?

MARTIN

You don't know who I *am* anymore.

BILLY

(*Flat*) No.

MARTIN

Well . . . neither does your mother.

BILLY

(*Trying to explain, but, still, rage underneath*) Parents fight; I
know that; all kids know that. There are good times and rot-

ten ones, and sometimes the blanket is pulled out from under
you, and . . .

MARTIN

(*Can't help saying it*) You're mixing your metaphors.

BILLY

(*Furious*) What!?

MARTIN

Never mind; probably not the best time to bring it up. You
were saying . . . "There are good times and rotten ones"?

BILLY

Yes. (*Quick sarcasm*) Thanks.

MARTIN

(*Noncommittal*) Welcome.

BILLY

But sometimes the whatever is pulled out from under you.

MARTIN

Rug, I think.

BILLY

Right! Now shut the fuck up! (MARTIN *opens his mouth, closes
it. Spits out*) Semanticist!

MARTIN

Very good! Where did you learn that?

BILLY

I go to a good school. Remember?

MARTIN

Yes, but still . . .

BILLY

I said, shut the fuck up!

MARTIN

(*Subsiding*) Right.

BILLY

There are good times, and there are rotten ones. There are times we are so . . . deep in content, in happiness, that we think we'll probably drown in it but we won't mind. There are *some* of those—not too many. There are times we don't know what the fuck's going on—*to* us, *with* us, *about* us —and that's most of the time. I'm talking about us so-called adolescents.

MARTIN

I know.

BILLY

And then there are the times we wish we were old enough to . . . just walk out the door and start all over again, somewhere else—blank it all out.

MARTIN

(*Quietly*) And this?

BILLY

(*Hard*) One guess, you *fuck*!! (*Huge*) What have you done with my *mother*!!??

MARTIN

(*Calm*) We finished our conversation (*gestures at ruined room*)—you see how we talk?—we finished our conversation, and she said a final . . . *thing*, and she left. She walked out, out the front door, slam.

BILLY

How long ago?

MARTIN

(*Shrugs*) An hour; maybe more; maybe two. I'm not very good at time and stuff right now.

BILLY

Two hours? And you haven't . . .

MARTIN

(*A little angry himself*) What!? called the police? (*Awful imitation of distress*) "Oh, Officer, help me! My wife just found out I've been doing it with livestock, and she's run off, and can you help me find her?" What!? Take off after her!? She's a grown woman; she could be having her hair done, for all I know.

BILLY

(*Dogged*) What did she *say* to you?

MARTIN

(*Rueful chuckle*) Oh . . . quite a few things.

BILLY

(*Bigger*) When she left! What did she say when she left!?

MARTIN

Something about . . . bringing me down—or whatever.

BILLY

Be specific.

MARTIN

Well, it's hard to be specific. We *were* busy after all, and . . .

BILLY

(*Big*) Exactly what she said, and *now*!

MARTIN

(*Clears his throat*) "You have brought me down, and . . . I will bring you down with me."

BILLY

(*Puzzled; trying to get it*) What does that *mean*?

MARTIN

(*Almost sweet*) No one's ever brought you down? No, I suppose not—not yet. It means . . . (*fails*) it means what it says:
that you have done to me what cannot be undone and . . . and
you won't get away with it.

(BILLY *stands for a moment and then spontaneously cries for a little, stops*)

BILLY

(*Wiping his eyes*) I see.

MARTIN

(*Further explanation*) You destroy me—I destroy you.

BILLY

Yes; I see. (*Indicates wreckage*) Then there's no point in set-
ting all this right.

MARTIN

(*Sad chuckle*) It does look pretty awful, *doesn't* it.

BILLY

Let's do it anyway.

MARTIN

Set the stage for the next round? (*Some self-pity and irony*)
Hunh! *What* next round!? It's all behind me, isn't it?—everything? All hope . . . all . . . "salvation"? (*Fast litany*) Dead-
end-rock-bottom-out-with-the-garbage-flushed-down-the-
toilet-ground-up-spit-out-over-the-edge with heavy weights,
down-down-sunk . . . whatever? All hope, everything? Gone?
Right?

BILLY

(*Shrugs*) Whatever. (BILLY *begins to right a few things, not
much; then quits*) What is it going to be then? Divorce?

MARTIN

(*Simply*) I don't know, Billy; I don't know that there are any
rules for where we are.

BILLY

Beyond all the rules, eh?

MARTIN

(*Some rue*) I think so.

BILLY

I wouldn't know. I guess I've never been in love. *Yet*, I mean.
Oh, lots of crushes, and all.

MARTIN

Only twice for me—your mother and . . . Sylvia.

BILLY

You're really holding onto this, *aren't* you.

MARTIN

To . . . ?

BILLY

(*Sneering*) This goat! This big love affair!

MARTIN

(*Shrugs*) It's true.

BILLY

Grow up!

MARTIN

Ah! Is *that* it! (BILLY *laughs, in spite of himself.* MARTIN *tries
to right a chair*) Help me with this. (BILLY *helps him*) Thanks!

BILLY

(*Shrugs*) Any time. (*Pause*) They asked us at school—when?
Last week, last month?—they asked each of us in this class to
talk about how normal our lives were, how . . . how conven-
tional it all was and how did we feel about it.

MARTIN

What kind of school *is* this!?

BILLY

(*Shrugs*) You chose it; you two chose it. And a lot of the guys
got up and talked about—you know—our home lives, how our
parents get on, and all; and it wasn't very special except the
guys whose parents are divorced or one has died or gone
crazy, or whatever.

MARTIN

Really? Crazy?

BILLY

Sure. Good private school. All guys, too; thanks. I mean, it was
all about what you'd expect. Maybe everybody left all the juicy
stuff out, or they didn't know it. (*Picks up a shard*) Where
does this go?

MARTIN

Trash, I suspect.

BILLY

(*Looks at it*) Too bad. (*Drops it*) So, it was all pretty dull,
pretty much what you'd expect.

MARTIN

I take it you haven't gotten up and spoken yet.

BILLY

(*Noncommittal*) Nope. Haven't. (*Waits a little*) You know what
I'm going to tell them—when I get up there on my hind legs?

MARTIN

(*Winces*) Do I *want* to know?

BILLY

Sure; you're a big guy.

MARTIN

I am diminished.

BILLY

Yeah? Well . . . whatever. I think what I'll tell them is this: that

I've been living with two people about as splendid as you can get; that if I'd been born to other people, it couldn't have been any better. (MARTIN *sighs heavily, puts a protesting hand up*) No; really; I mean it. You two guys are about as good as they come. You're smart, and fair, and you have a sense of humor —both of you—and . . . and you're Democrats. You *are* Democrats, aren't you?

MARTIN

More than *they* are, sometimes.

BILLY

That's what I thought, and you've figured out that raising a kid does *not* include making him into a carbon copy of *you*, that you're letting me think you're putting up with me being gay far better than you probably really are.

MARTIN

Oh, now . . .

BILLY

Thank you, by the way.

MARTIN

It's the least.

BILLY

(*Nodding*) Right.

MARTIN

(*Feigned surprise*) You're *gay*!?

BILLY

(*Smiles*) Shut up. Anyway, you've let me have it better than a lot of kids, better than a lot of "Moms and Dads" have, a lot closer to what being grown up will look like—as far as I can tell. Good guidance; it's great to see how two people can love each other . . .

MARTIN

Don't!

BILLY

At least that's what I thought—until yesterday, until the shit hit the fan!

MARTIN

Billy, please don't.

BILLY

(*Big crying underneath*) . . . until the shit hit the fan, and the talk I was going to do at school became history. (*Exaggerated*) What will I say *now*!? Goodness me! The Good Ship Lollipop has gone and sunk. (*More normal tone*) What will I say!? Well, let's see: I came home yesterday and everything had been great—absolutely normal, therefore great. Great parents, great house, great trees, great cars—you know: the old "great." (*Bigger now, more exaggerated*) But then today I come home, and what do I *find*? I find my great Mom and my great Dad talking about a letter from great good friend Ross . . .

MARTIN

(*Deep anger*) Fuck Ross!!

BILLY

Yes? A letter from great good friend Ross written to great good Mom about how great good Dad has been out in the barnyard fucking *animals*!!

MARTIN

Don't . . . *do* this.

BILLY

Animals! Well, one in particular. A goat! A fucking goat! You see, guys, your stories are swell or whatever, but I've got one'll knock your socks off, as they used to say, wipe the tattoos right off your butts. Ya see, while great old Mom and great old Dad have been doing the great old parent thing, one of them has been underneath the house, down in the cellar, digging a pit so deep!, so wide!, so . . . HUGE! . . . we'll all fall in and (*crying now*) and never . . . be . . . able . . . to . . . climb . . . out . . . again—no matter how much we want to, how hard we

try. And you see, kids, fellow students, you see, I love these
people. I love the man who's been down there digging—when
he's not giving it to a goat! I love this man! I love him! (*Drops
whatever he's holding, moves to* MARTIN, *arms out*) I love
him! (*Wraps his arms around* MARTIN, *who doesn't know
what to do. Starts kissing* MARTIN *on the hands, then on the
neck, crying the while. Then it turns—or does it?—and he
kisses* MARTIN *full on the mouth—a deep, sobbing, sexual kiss.*
ROSS *has entered, stands watching.* MARTIN *tries to disengage
from* BILLY, *but* BILLY *moans, holds on. Finally* MARTIN
shoves him away. BILLY *stands there, still sobbing, arms
around nothing. They have not seen* ROSS.)

MARTIN

Don't *do* that!!

BILLY

I *love* you!

MARTIN

Sure you do, you . . . you . . .

BILLY

Faggot? You faggot?

MARTIN

(*Enraged*) That's not what I was going to say!!

BILLY

(*So sad; so sincere*) Dad! I *love* you! Hold me! Please!

MARTIN

(*Holds him; strokes him*) Shhhhhh; shhhh; shhhhh now.

BILLY

(*Disengaging finally*) I'm sorry; I didn't mean to . . .

MARTIN

No; it's all right. (*Arms out*) Here; let me hold you.
(BILLY *moves to him again; a momentary silent embrace*)

ROSS

Excuse me. (*They are startled, split. Maybe* BILLY *stumbles over something.*) I'm sorry; I didn't mean to interrupt your little . . .

MARTIN

(*Cold fury*) What!? See a man and his son kissing? That would go nicely in one of your fucking letters. Judas! Get out of here!

BILLY

(*To* ROSS) It wasn't what you think!

MARTIN

(*At* BILLY) Yes! Yes, it was! Don't apologize. (*To* ROSS) Too bad you couldn't have brought your fucking TV crew over! Don't you and *your* son ever kiss? Don't you and—what's his name? —*Todd* love one another?

ROSS

(*Hard; contemptuous*) Not *that* way!

MARTIN

(*Angry and reckless*) *That* way!? *What* way!? (*Points vigorously at* BILLY) This boy is hurt! I've hurt him, and he still loves me! You fucker! He loves his father, and if it . . . clicks over and becomes—what?—sexual for . . . just a moment . . . so what!? So fucking what!? He's hurt and he's lonely and mind your own fucking business!

ROSS

(*A sneer*) You're sicker than I thought.

MARTIN

No! I'm hysterical!

BILLY

(*Rueful wonder*) It *did.* It clicked over, and you were just another . . .

MARTIN

It's all right.

BILLY

. . . another man. I get confused . . . sex and love; loving
and . . . (*To* ROSS) I probably *do* want to sleep with him.
(*Rueful laugh*) I want to sleep with everyone.

MARTIN

(*To quiet him*) It's all right.

BILLY

(*Still to* ROSS) Except you, probably.

ROSS

Jesus! Sick! What is it . . . contagious?

BILLY

(*Confused*) What? Is what?

MARTIN

(*Moves over to comfort* BILLY) There was a man told me
once—a friend; we went to the same gym—he told me he
had his kid on his lap one day—not even old enough to be a
boy or a girl: a baby—and he had . . . *it* on his lap, and it was
gurgling at him and making giggling sounds, and he had it
with his arms around it, (*demonstrates*) in his lap, shifting it a
little from side to side to make it happier, to make it giggle
more . . . and all at once he realized he was getting hard.

ROSS

Jesus!

BILLY

Oh my God . . .

MARTIN

. . . that the baby in his lap was making him hard—not arous-
ing him; it wasn't sexual, but it was happening.

ROSS

Jesus!

MARTIN

. . . his dick was rising to the baby in his lap—his baby; his lap. And when he realized what was happening, he thought he would die; his pulse was going a mile a minute; his ears were ringing—loud! Very *loud*! And he was going to faint; he *knew* it, and then the moment passed, and he knew it had all been an accident, that it meant . . . nothing—that nothing was connected to anything else. His wife came in; she smiled; he smiled and handed her the baby. And that was it; it was over. (*Shrugs*) Things happen. Besides—I'm hysterical. Remember?

ROSS

What are you doing? *Defending* yourself?! Jesus. You're sick.

MARTIN

(*Contempt*) Do you have any other words? Sick and Jesus? Is that all you have?

BILLY

(*Shy*) Was it me? Was it me, Dad? Was the baby me?

MARTIN

(*To* BILLY; *after a pause; gently*) Hush.

BILLY

(*Almost frightened*) Was it?

MARTIN

(*Turning to* ROSS) So, what do you want here now, mother-fucker!? Judas!?

ROSS

Stevie called—what? An hour ago? More? She said you needed me; she said to come over.

MARTIN

I don't! Get out! (*Surprise*) She *called* you?

ROSS

Yes. (*Shakes his head*) Getting hard with a baby! Is there anything you people don't get off on!?

BILLY

(*Once more*) Was it, Dad?

MARTIN

(*So clearly a lie; gently*) Of course not, Billy. (*To* ROSS; *hard, eyes narrowing*) Is there anything "we people" don't get off on? Is there anything anyone doesn't get off on, whether we admit it or not—whether we *know* it or not? Remember Saint Sebastian with all the arrows shot into him? He probably came! God knows the faithful did! Shall I go on!? You want to hear about the cross!?

BILLY

(*Quietly; smiling*) No, of course it wasn't . . . wasn't me.

ROSS

(*Shaking his head; sad, but with a lip curled*) Sick; sick; sick.

MARTIN

(*At* ROSS; *growing rage*) I'll tell you what's sick! Writing that fucking letter to Stevie—why doesn't matter!!—that's what's sick! I *tell* you about it; I share it with you, the . . . the . . . whole . . . awful . . . thing, because I think I've lost it, maybe; I *tell* you; I *share* it with you because you're . . . what!? . . . you're my best friend in the whole world? Because I needed to tell *somebody*, somebody with his head on straight enough to hear it? I *tell* you, and you fucking turn around and . . .

ROSS

I *had* to!!

MARTIN

No! You *didn't*! You didn't *have* to!

ROSS

(*Dogmatic*) I couldn't let you *continue*!

MARTIN

(*Near tears*) I could have worked it out. I could have stopped, and no one would have known. Except you, motherfucker. Mister one strike and you're out. I could have . . .

ROSS

No! You couldn't!

MARTIN

I could have worked it out! And now nothing can *ever* be put back together! *Ever!*

BILLY

(*Trying to help*) Dad . . .

MARTIN

(*Savage*) You shut up! (BILLY *winces.* MARTIN *reacts*) Oh, God! I'm sorry. (*To* ROSS) Yes; all right, it *was* sick, and yes, it *was* compulsive, and . . .

ROSS

IS! Not *was*! IS!

MARTIN

(*Stopped in his tracks*) I . . . I . . .

ROSS

IS!

MARTIN

(*Gathering himself*) Is. All right. *Is. Is* sick; *is* compulsive.

ROSS

(*Pushing*) And it was *wrong!*

MARTIN

It was . . . it was . . . what?

ROSS

Wrong! Deeply, destructively *wrong!*

MARTIN

Whatever you want. (*Rage growing*) But I could have handled it! You didn't have to bring it all down! You didn't have to destroy both of us; you didn't have to destroy Stevie, too!

ROSS

Me!? *Me* bring you down!? This isn't . . . embezzlement, honey; this isn't stealing from helpless widows; this isn't going to whores and coming down with the clap, or whatever, you know. This isn't the stuff that stops a career in its tracks for a little while—humiliation, public remorse, and then back up again. This is *beyond* that—*way* beyond it! You go on and you'll slip up one day. Somebody'll see you. Somebody'll surprise you one day, in whatever barn you put her in, no matter where you put her. Somebody'll see you, on your knees behind the damn animal; your pants around your ankles. Somebody will *catch* you at it.

BILLY

Let him alone. For God's sake, Ross . . .

ROSS

(*Waving* BILLY *off; to* MARTIN) Do you know there are prison terms for this? Some states they kill you for it? Do you know what they'd *do* to you. The press? Everybody? Down it all comes—your career; your life . . . everything. (*So cold; so rational*) For fucking a goat. (*Shakes his head sadly;* BILLY *is weeping quietly*)

MARTIN

(*Long pause*) Is *that* what it is, then? That people will *know*!? That people will find *out*!? That I can do whatever I want, and that's what matters!? That people will find *out*!? Fuck the . . . thing it*self*!? Fuck what it *means*!? That people will find *out*!?

ROSS

Your soul is your own business. The rest I can *help* you with.

MARTIN

Of course it's my business, and clearly you don't have one.

ROSS

(*Mild interest*) Oh?

MARTIN

So that's what it comes down to, eh? . . . what we can get away with?

ROSS

Sure.

MARTIN

(*Heavy irony*) Oh, thank God! It's so simple! I thought it was
. . . I thought it had to do with love and loss, and it's only about
. . . getting *by*. Well, Stevie and I have been wrestling with the
wrong angel! When she comes back—*if* she comes back—I'll
have to set her straight about what matters. (*Intense; not looking at* ROSS *or* BILLY; *pounding his hands on his knees perhaps*) Does nobody understand what happened!?

ROSS

Oh, for Christ's sake, Martin!

BILLY

Dad . . .

MARTIN

(*Crying a little*) Why can't anyone understand this . . . that I
am *alone* . . . all . . . *alone*!

(*A silence. Then we hear a sound at the door.*)

BILLY

Mom? (BILLY *going into the hall. Gone.*)

MARTIN

(*Pause; to* ROSS, *begging*) You *do* understand; *don't* you.

ROSS

(*Long pause; shakes his head*) No.

(STEVIE *is dragging a dead goat. The goat's throat is cut; the blood is down*
STEVIE's *dress, on her arms. She stops*)

ROSS

Oh, my God.

MARTIN

What have you done!?

STEVIE

Here.

BILLY

(*Generally; to no one; helpless; a quiet plea*) Help. Help.

ROSS

Oh, my God.

(MARTIN *moves toward* STEVIE)

MARTIN

What have you done!? Oh, my God, what have you *done*!?

(BILLY *is crying.* STEVIE *regards* MARTIN *for a moment;* ROSS *is immobile.*)

STEVIE

(*Turns to face him; evenly, without emotion*) I went where
Ross told me I would find . . . your friend. I found her. I killed
her. I brought her here to you. (*Odd little question*) No?

MARTIN

(*A profound cry*) ANNNNNNH!

STEVIE

Why are you surprised? What did you expect me to do.

MARTIN

(*Crying*) What did she *do*!? What did she ever *do*!? (*To* STEVIE)
I ask you: what did she ever *do*!?

STEVIE

(*Pause; quietly*) She loved you . . . you say. As much as *I* do.

MARTIN

(*To* STEVIE; *empty*) I'm sorry. (*To* BILLY; *empty*) I'm sorry.
(*Then . . .*) I'm sorry.

BILLY

(*To one, then the other; no reaction from them*) Dad? Mom?

(*Tableau*)

End